UNICORN SHIT IS STILL SHIT

Delphine Van Eyck

Presentation by *BookLeaf Publishing*

Web: www.bookleafpub.com

E-mail: info@bookleafpub.com

ISBN: 978-93-95890-20-5

First edition 2022

To my big sister, who reminded me that the unbearable calvary of life always has an end. Thank you

ACKNOWLEDGEMENT

A big thank you to BookLeaf Publishing, without whom I would never have made the bet to publish my first written work.

The Innocence of the Baby Unicorn

It is very heartbreaking to witness a newborn come into this life. Childbirth is for me the darkest day you can think of. Seeing mothers in heaven with their baby in their arms upsets me. Various feelings are intertwined in me, ranging from hatred to helplessness, through affliction and distress. And above all: the feeling of looking at the selfishness of someone who should know better.

The pride of creating a life to leave a trace of our passage here saddens me as much as it revolts me. Do humans have no conscience? Our kind is a failure. We have ruined our own environment. We hurt each other. We are the source of so much torment. And you would like to add to this infernal mess?

Once our childlike purity is lost, we never regain it. Then you willingly condemn another human being to lose it too, consoling yourself for the fact that your offspring will have lived a few years of "pure" innocence. What right do you have to put a child in such a depraved world?

Are you not capable of being selfless enough to suffer alone? Do you not love children enough not to have any, and thus avoid the inevitable series of disappointments that will follow in their lives?

The Lost Innocence of the Unicorn

I consider every parent a self-absorbed wretch, and I have long resented you, Mother, for that. I now have to live with a lot of trauma, with the memory of everyone who hurt me. I have to keep moving forward without knowing the purpose of my existence and asking myself a thousand unresolved questions. Who thinks you did me a favor by giving birth to me?

With your bullshit, I will rather have to deal with a world that heats up and that will no longer suit me. While you quietly die of old age, I will look the reaper in the eye with no way to escape. I will see my death in the face and I will disappear.

Except now, I am no longer a sweet oblivious kid. I know that death can only be accompanied by pain and fear. It is all because of you, Mother, and your decision to have me. I hope my few years of innocence have been worth it for you, because now that they are forever shattered, I have plenty of room in my heart to fill it with rancor towards you.

There is no Unicorn in Hell

Last night, I dreamed about you, Mother. That is all I allow myself with regard to you. Not that you are actually dead, of course, but you are to me. I buried you long ago, deep in my miserable and heartbreaking memories.

I remember as a child looking up and meeting your eyes so full of contempt for me that I could recognize the disgust on your face. You made it clear to me that you never wanted me in your home.

After years of looking for love, or at least elementary maternal respect, I saw with despair that I would never obtain it. At a time when I thought I could no longer be hurt by your self-centeredness and narcissistic attitude again, you still managed to do the unthinkable.

You tried to destroy the life I had with a woman worth a thousand times more than you. Out of jealousy, resentment? What do I know? And I don't care anymore. You died the day I decided to choose her, with her big heart in her tiny silhouette.

You died when I promised to marry this woman who supported me, esteemed me, but above all, loved me with all her soul. I learned with her that unconditional love is indeed unconditional. A fairly simple concept that I should have learned from an early age, although it does not seem like I was taught it.

So I pray now. Every day. So that you stay away from me and my happiness. I know karma exists and will take care of you. Satan has already warmed your seat in hell. I'm just waiting for the day you actually die. I hope this underworld really exists so you can burn in it for eternity, and I will sleep peacefully with the smile of a sinner who had a good day.

Time Does Not Affect Unicorns

We win it, we lose it, but we never get it back. It slips through our fingers, as it is impossible to restrain it. It is friend or foe, but it always affects us. We see its effects on our faces, yet it remains invisible. It goes slowly, it goes fast, brings us joy or makes us suffer. We can never own it, but every day we deal with it. We are part of it, but unlike us, it will never die. It will continue on his way long after our death, always in the same direction. Changing its course is inconceivable. It is the only remedy for all our heartaches, but also often the cause. It breaks down into fractions or can last for eternity. As far as we are concerned, we have very little moment to spend with it, so let's do everything to enjoy it while we are alive.

Unicorn Utopia

I would like the past not to exist. That there is no collective memory. I can already hear the optimists object that it is essential! That history allows us to learn and not repeat the same mistakes. If only it was true. War has existed since the dawn of time. We did nothing. Poverty has always been before our eyes. We did nothing. Why would we? This suits those who take advantage of the system. Now imagine a clean slate. A brain that starts afresh. We would have no idea of the old patterns. Everyone would have the same chances. We would live as if we were starting over from the beginning, with no history of conflict, racism or religious drift. We would act as if we were meeting the world for the first time, and that everything would have to be built. Would we be different? Or would it be a utopia to hope that we can do better?

Good Old Times with Unicorns

When I was young
I used to be gone all day
I was pedaling on my bicycle
Like a real grown-up
I had fun with friends

Wind in the face
We had this freedom
To do impossible things together
Until our mothers, feigning concern
Came looking for us in the alley

They were also shouting
Through the open window
For us to come inside
Then we ate the hot stew
And savored the best pie

We told them which monsters we had killed
Which princesses we had saved
Oh! The innocence of our young years
"Never accept candy from strangers"
And we were ready to face the world

I do not want to put a young one
In this unpredictable world anymore
As the list of dangers goes on
Sadly, I am not equipped
To prevent them all

A Dad to his Daughter Unicorn

I would like to tell you that you are beautiful
I would like you to show me how strong you are
I would like to share with you my pride in
raising an intelligent woman like you
I would like to promise you a world where you
can do whatever you want

Instead, I claim there are some that shine
brighter than you
I pretend that anyone could break you like a rag
doll
I remind you that men do not want to feel
threatened by intelligence
And that life is a bitch controlled by males who
won't let you be yourself

I have indeed used all the worst schemes of our
despicable society
So that you refrain from opening wide your
wings
To fly too high, the fall is more brutal
To keep you safe, I would lie to you again

I preferred to protect you from this psychotic
world
At the risk of sounding like a misogynist
The love I have for you is more powerful than
anything
I'm sorry to have disappointed you, but I would
do it again

Oh! I saw the hate you had for me
Please do not think I will ever forgive myself
It was the impossible choice I had to make
To preserve you from the worst in man

Cutie Pie Unicorn

Sleep tight Cutie Pie
The night is so peaceful
Pull the duvet up under your nose
Then close your little fairy eyes
Nothing can happen to you

What is that strange noise?
Nothing to worry about
Daddy came into your room
To keep watching
He will take care of the monster under the bed

Sleep well Cutie Pie
You are safe now
Can you feel daddy's gentle caress
Here to reassure you?
Such a warm presence

Go back to the land of dreams and unicorns
Your wild imagination is at its peak at night
A hand in your blond hair
You calm down right away
Until the fingers stiffen and tighten

A fear never felt before
But yet never forgotten
Sounds of monsters under the bed
Has become the least of your worries
Who said monsters hide?

The Introvert Unicorn

In the quiet night
The eerie sound of silence
Yet liberating

An erratic crowd
The introvert mourns his loss —
Beloved loneliness

Hiding with a mask
While smiling at everyone
Because life hurts me

Erasing myself —
No one sees me anymore
Nor remember me

Waiting for something
When do I know what it is?
My life is pointless

Insignificant
Is how God created me —
How evil is that?

If Only Mirrors Could Reflect Unicorns

Mirrors are aimless and destructive. They never helped humanity to change any perspective. Indeed, virtuous individuals would observe constantly the oppression of their soul by bodily dictates. How not to lose faith? As tears stream down their cheeks, their eyes fail to see the breathtaking beauty of their worth. The mirror reflects nothing but the features we have had since birth. This says nothing of the purity of heart, nor of the rich interiority of our next generations. As society bombards us with complexes, unscrupulous leaders revel in their reflection. Impossible for them to notice all the darkness of their corrupted soul when they have in front of them the smiling face of the victorious. I am not overstating anything when I come to this consensus: mirrors are futile and should not exist.

Marginalized Unicorn

Unleash your marginality
As to quench your thirst
Drinking on the edge of the World
Crying a sea of ignoramuses
Head held high
So as not to drown

Modern times though
Prefer to riddle with bullets
What bothers
A pellets wave
The loss of a friend
Troubled soul

Tears flood our eyes
Like the waves of the ocean
We cry at the Requiem, Fate laughs
Laughs at those we love
In connivance with Death
Who delights herself

At the Last Judgment
Devotees of hate will not be innocent
Their hands stained with blood
Of those they pretend not to know

And not see
Hypocrisy

Fortuna is sometimes evil
But do not leave anything to chance
Stay undefeated
Pride on the forehead
Love on the lips
You will not be forgotten

My Unicorn Skin in the Wind

As soon as you get closer
I fade away
Do not lay eyes on me
I will vanish anyway

My body is a prison
My scars the fissures
Not gaping enough
To escape quietly

I am locked in this flesh
That I do not recognize
Indeed, I am still surprised
When I see my own reflection

I would like to remove my skin
I would like to hang this skin in the wind
And beat it to love it true
Then put it back, just to feel

Will this skin be cleaner?
Will I forget the dirty hands that outraged it?
Will my lips ever be able to stretch enough
To bring a smile back to this life?

Power to Female Unicorns

As long as women are not in power
Do not expect anything from humanity
We thought we were in a modern age
Where wars have been eradicated. How funny

As long as there are men in power
It is better to not expect anything
Only men know how to waste resources
Without benefiting his neighbor

Welcome to a world
Where Ukraine is dying
Women are crying and crossing their fingers
Men are laughing and crossing their arms

Those in power do not react
Unless it affects their own interest
We should have more Finland, Germany and
Sweden
And fewer supreme courts run by white men

I no longer expect any advances in human rights
Sure, why not let the Taliban handle it
Why not let North Korea isolate its people
And starve them to death?

A hundred reasons are good to fight
However, when we talk about preserving human
dignity
Leaders think twice
It is definitely not paying enough

Every political movement is interested
But not in the right priorities
Fundamental rights? Resource equity?
Education?
No thanks, we prefer to ensure universal access
to weapons

We forgive the rapists
And condemn those who abort
I am begging you, we need women in power
It is our only chance to repent

A Unicorn in a Fairy Tale

Sorry to break it to you, but a fairy tale is not a happy story that has come to an end. These are unfinished stories. If life was all about having kids and getting married, we would know. Do not get me wrong, I understand that everything is there to amaze the eyes of hundreds of little girls. Simply, a few small passages have been eluded to make the whole thing much more glamorous than it is in real life. We are made to believe that we can "vivre d'amour et d'eau fraîche". Well, I guess they will never mention the fact that the princess will have the mental load all to herself until the end of her life. Without ever complaining, she will have to take care of the progeniture, of the whole castle and of her husband as if he were unable to meet his own basic needs. Because Sir has to do significant things, talk to important people, and make sure his wife is financially dependent so he can have any use in the household. If behind every great man there is a woman, behind every great woman there is only herself. Because that is what we have been doing for centuries now...

A Strong Unicorn Holds Back Tears

I walk alone
I move at full speed
To be safe

What is new?
I was touched without consent
And kept smiling

In my prison
I scrub all the floors
Cell is clean

Cleaning is done
The meal is on the table
Out of danger

Really?

Do not Cry
It would be much worse
Lower your eyes

Closing my eyes
Taking the blows without flinching
Clenching my teeth

A "stray" bullet
Her body on the bed
An open wound

Unicorns Need Trust

It is extremely painful
To be a social entity
Who nevertheless
Does not trust his contemporary

I dread every face I meet
I imagine them hiding in the shadows
Fake smiles stretching a mouth
That only learned to tell half-truths

I do not trust anyone anymore
I assume you have bad intentions
It is less disappointing
When I get betrayed

Why having contact with humans
When beasts spread love
Without knowing disloyalty
That is why I blindly trust them

Happiness is a Unicorn Shit

Here is what I think. Happiness is like unicorn shit. We do not really know if it exists. Sometimes I thought I was getting close to it, I even thought I had reached it. And what followed? Nothingness, or even more depressing than that, the everyday life and routine. I am happy for a few hours, then fall back into comforting neutrality at best, dark thoughts at worst. It is not sustainable. I feel like I have to find a way to experience happy events one after another so that I can make a positive chain for myself, long enough to be designated as a moment of happiness.

So what did I learn from my experience? That even unicorn shit is still just shit. I may be excited for a moment and then realize that life is still what it was. I miss when I was young, when everything around me was a source of pleasure and laughter. Now that my brain has made almost all the connections, it is well aware of the dreary world we live in. Then, I am just waiting for the fabulous senility that will bring me back to childhood to arrive, so I can forget this life

and still marvel at a ladybug and dream of
unicorns.

26

Despair of the Unicorn

27

Why does vile remain? —
Bad things already exist
Don't we have enough?

Never show distress
Or you will be much abused —
The wolf has long teeth

Painful existence —
A series of encounters
Birth, life, and sweet death

Joy has flown away
My misery tears the night
In silence I cry

With desperate heart
Sadness will get the better
Of you, me, and us

Suffer in silence
Endure the unthinkable —
Will this ever end?

I beg my friend Death
The only one who knows me
To deliver me

Extinction of the Unicorn

Green singing cricket
Feeling of grass underfoot
The calm of the night

A breeze in the hair
The tender smile of a child —
Enjoy while it lasts

Being nostalgic —
The memory of the past
Fear of the future

Nurturing nature
We hear the song of the bird
And cut down the tree

What absurdity
Without remorse we destroy —
Life will not grow back

Toxic pollution
Don't be surprised by sick men
With their lungs blackened

Unbearable heat
Drought is never far away
Gaia is ruthless

The sea will dry up
The volcano will wake up —
Extinction of life

A Unicorn in Heaven

Kneeling between the graves
Eyes closed, mouth shut
Stand up is for the braves
I just do not have the gut

Here I am, staring at your epitaph
Without ever blinking
Sadly, I would like to laugh
At what life brings

So many beautiful flowers
In such a grim place
Please God, give me the power
To dry my tears apace

Somehow, I envy your fate
To perish and rest in peace
Please let me ornate
The symbol of your release

You are free now
We have to bear our grief
I will never stop to bow
To your faith and belief

I should have said I love you
But I preferred to flee
I am a coward who left you
When you needed me

I know it is up to me
To overcome my demons
For you I will plant a tree
Which will bloom under your sun

Time for me to say goodbye
Trying to forget my own guilt
Never I wanted you to die
Yet I have a life to get built

The Contradictions of the Unicorn

Have you ever wanted
To live and die
At the same time?

To go to sleep
And dream
Of never waking up again?

I would like to no longer
Have the ability to think
It makes us unhappy

I admire the simple-minded
Who finds happiness
In the little things

The thing is
They just do not see
That destruction is coming

Often I want silence
But when it goes on
I get anxious

I want to stay in the shadows
But to feel that I exist
And have light around me

Get away from me
But come closer
I need you to stay with me

I want everything
And I do not want anything
Maybe I just want this to end for good